HAREF
DURI ᴎ ᴏ
THE FIRST WORLD
WAR
1914-1918

Tanya Britton

ISBN
978-0-9571807-4-1

Contents

INTRODUCTION

The name 'Harefield' is thought to have been derived from 'open land used by an army'. The village dates back to before the survey of Domesday and lay within the hundred of Elthorne. There were three manors in Harefield – Harefield itself and the sub-manor of Brackenbury and Moorhall.

During the late 18th century the Grand Union Canal opened and contributed to Harefield's expansion. By the turn of the 20th century in 1901, the village was still developing and by the eve of war had sufficiently developed to allow Harefield to play an important part in the daily struggles which any war can bring.

My thanks are extended to the Local History Library staff at Uxbridge Library for their co-operation, Stephen Britton and Eric Button.

Every reasonable care had been taken in compiling this document. Responsibility cannot be accepted for any errors or omissions.

SETTING THE SCENE

Harefield's history goes back a very long way. Harefield was mentioned in the Domesday Book as was its Church, dedicated to St. Mary. Part of the nave dates from the 12th century. Moor Hall dated back to the 13th century, although within it lay a house of the 12th century (a camera, and is used to denote the smaller houses of the Order of St. John) of the Knights Hospitallers of St. John of Jerusalem. It was demolished in 1961.

Harefield Parish Church (Hillingdon Local Studies, Archives and Museum Service)

Moving on in time, a number of large houses had been constructed in the 16th century. Dairy House (later Dewes Farm) was known to have been built prior to 1602 when Queen Elizabeth I was entertained here.

The period between 1902 when the Boer War had ended and the beginning of the Great War in August 1914 was one of peace and comparative economic stability, but not advance, although the period was a time of war scares. July was the time for holidays, this year the most brilliant summer for years, and August the time of annual training. The Territorial Army, and many of its units were already mustered in camp whilst others were about to go into camp that weekend. The local 'E' Company, 8th Middlesex V.B. Regiment was on the outbreak of war at Salisbury Plain for its annual training. It had been there since July.

Park Lane, Harefield
(Hillingdon Local Studies. Archives and Museum Service)

Although the suburban expansion of London in the nineteenth century was great and high rents were forcing workers to move to cheaper areas and commute, in some instances the population had doubled in the space of seven years, the modern London Borough of Hillingdon was still largely unaffected by this spread. In 1895 it was noted that the occupants of the crowded cottages suffered from serious debilitating illnesses. In that year, building land was advertised for sale in Northwood Road. The population in Harefield in 1901 was 2008, by 1911 was 2402, rising only slightly in 1912 to 2450 with a larger increase the following year, making a total of 2530 people.

The 1911 census showed that one-tenth of the population of England was living in overcrowded conditions and it was estimated that between 5 and 10% of urban workmen were living in slums. By 1912 there had been a growing awareness of the problems created since 1851 by London's rapid expansion. The new Housing Act of 1909 vested powers in Local Authorities to, should they wish, prepare town-planning schemes. Plans had been announced by the Cavendish Land Company to develop Harefield Place as a high-class housing estate in June 1914. There was a housing scheme at Harefield, where negotiations had taken place with Mr. Billyard Leake in regard to land, who was willing to accept the Council's offer of £215 an acre for the land (5 acres) not far from the Council Schools and opening out into Park Lane.

When the Grand Union Canal was built alongside the River Colne in 1797, lime-kilns and copper-mills soon appeared and by the end of the 19th century Harefield had begun to change from its rural environment. By the end of the 19th century brickmaking employed a large number of youngsters who were paid higher wages than those engaged on agricultural or domestic work. The principal crop was hay which was taken to London either by barge from the wharf at Moor Hall, or by road. Paper mills had existed in Harefield since 1674 In the middle of the 18th century the mills were leased to the Mines Royal Company who converted the mills to work copper in 1802. In 1870 Mr. Thomas Newell bought the mill and it became a paper mill again for the manufacture of envelopes. When he became bankrupt in 1897, the lease was taken over by the United Asbestos Company, although asbestos mills had started in 1882 and a cement works opened in 1886 on the site of former brickworks. The Breakspear Institute which had been founded in 1896 and was mainly used as a working men's club, was in need of extending. By the early 20th century, however, there were still 20 farms in the area, although the Agricultural Depression of the 1870s and 1880s saw a rapid turnover of tenancies and some farmers turned to dairy farming to supply London with milk. Here the tranquillity of the place also attracted visitors. Mrs. Gough had established tea-rooms in the High Street where she gave every attention to cyclists and other travellers and at the 'Halfway House' angling permits could be bought from the proprietress, Mrs. Watkins.

A school had existed at Harefield for a number of years and in 1871 a separate infant school was opened in the Memorial Hall, with another schoolroom added in 1879. A temporary co-educational school was opened in 1904 in a temporary building which was replaced in 1908.

Harefield's workhouse which had been established before 1776, closed in 1836. At Hillingdon, the dreaded workhouse, which had opened in 1747 was enlarged in 1838 to become the workhouse for Cowley, Hayes, Hillingdon and

Uxbridge, West Drayton, Ruislip, Ickenham and Harefield. At one period in 1911 there had been as many as 282 unfortunate inmates, although for the following years the numbers tended to be less. In 1930 it became part of Hillingdon Hospital.

The Rose and Crown Public House at Harefield (Hillingdon Local Studies, Archives and Museum Service)

The provision of social activities to meet the expansion of population after 1890 proceeded at a slow rate. However, some sports clubs had started before the turn of the 20th century, including several cricket teams. Harefield United Football Club was the oldest in Middlesex and started in 1868. Harefield Football Club was founded as the Breakspear Institute Club in 1896 and there was also an athletic institution and a boxing club which were both in existence prior to 1914.

The European situation was getting blacker, although the impasse of Home Rule for Ireland was predominant in people's minds. War clouds were looming……….

WAR IS DECLARED…

The declaration of War between Austria and Serbia on 29th July 1914 seemed sudden. All hopes of peace were gradually abandoned and on the morning of 4th August 1914 Britain declared war on Germany. The announcement was greeted with relief by many. The War would be over by Christmas, the 'Hun' taught a lesson and victory would be won. Patriotic fervour was the order of the day.

Banks closed and crowds of panic-stricken people flocked to all the local shops to buy food and provisions and as many goods as they could carry and found that prices were rising. Local provision shops opened far beyond their usual closing times. Although the Government maximum-price scheme quickly put a stop to it, the price of sugar, most of which had hitherto been imported from German and Austria, immediately went up and the Government had to issue suggested prices for it and hoarding was made a criminal offence. As delivery boys went off to war, so people went in person to shop and provision shops stayed open long after usual closing times.

Within hours, the suffragettes put their aims on hold. Leaders of the women's suffrage movement supported the war effort, urging men to enlist and women to work in industry, preferring to put temporally aside their cause. It also worked to combat the appalling poverty suffered by ordinary people.

Every farm had its hayricks commandeered by the War Department, leaving only the bare minimum. Hay was baled by the Pioneer Corps and taken away to Cavalry depots. The authorities had lists of all tradesmen and others who were likely to be able to furnish draught and other horses and the War Office commandeered several horses from local traders.

Local Councils, along with other employers, found business difficult with prices rising, supplies drying up, men joining up and transport being requisitioned by the Government, but quickly set up Emergency Committees for arranging relief measures for those on active service. The first local one was at Uxbridge, which included Hillingdon East, Cowley, Ickenham and Harefield, shortly followed by almost every town and village in the district.

Several traders cancelled their contracts with the Council as their supplies had dried up. Council employees were guaranteed their jobs if and when they returned from the war. They also were to receive the wages they earned when they left the Council to join up, minus their Army, Navy or Air Force pay.

The conflict, which was to be one of the greatest in the history of the world, was to grow to involve the whole population.

EMPLOYMENT

By the second week of war, the future for the industries based at Harefield looked bleak and many unfounded rumours circulated. In some cases men were turned away because of the lack of work, others were working three-quarter time, while others were working three days a week and some half days only. Workers at the Bells' United Asbestos Factory were working short weeks as were the employees of the Poilite Factory who had ceased making Poilite when war broke out because of the difficulty of transport and intended not to begin making it again until the war was ended. Their workers were employed on other work. As a consequence of this, part of the Cement Works began working half time, but the rubber department still worked full-time as it had urgent Admiralty orders to fulfill.

WELCOME SURPRISE FOR HAREFIELD WORKS.

In consequence of the increase in food prices due to the war, and the hardships occasioned thereby, the directors of Bell's Asbestos Ltd., have decided, until further notice, to give workers a temporary " food bonus " as follows :—3s. per week for married men, receiving 25s. or less ; 2s. per week for all other workers. No bonus will be paid to any worker for the week during which he or she may leave, nor if they have not worked full time, unless through causes beyond their control, and satisfactory to the Works Managers. The Managing Directors in announcing the above, took the opportunity of thanking the employees for their special endeavours since the war to increase the output so essential for Government purposes, and reminded them that only high rates of output, maximum time, minimum waste, and the greatest economy in every department enabled the Company to cope with the present situation. Everyone is aware that raw material is now at such prices that waste must be avoided with the utmost care.

This is one of the kind of steps which gives employees an interest in the business, and in some very small degree a profit-sharing standing.

How the news of the surprise reached the public (Gazette Newspapers)

Within days of the outbreak of war, schemes were set up locally to take any necessary steps for safeguarding public welfare. However, the initial rise in unemployment and poverty was brief and as the war continued the demand for war material increased. In 1915, the Metropolitan Munitions Committee was set up in Kingsway to further the output of war material in the Metropolitan area, which was divided into areas. Its brief was to determine what in each district was capable of production, obtaining help from suitable traders and others, as well as determining which new works or shops should be rented or bought. They also had full powers to rent lathes, machine tools, presses etc of those at that time who were engaged on civil work in the Metropolitan area, but any purchase had to be agreed with the Ministry of Munitions.

Gradually many existing factories converted all or part of their production lines to the making of war materials. Many of them made very extensive additions, the like of which would not have been seen but for the urgent requirements of the war departments. Local saddlers made harnesses and motor car shops and the engineers obtained contracts suitable to their line of work. Every available lathe was put to turning shells - if an employer was willing to use his lathe for that purpose he was allowed to keep it in his own workshop and employ his own workers, if not his lathe was commandeered and taken off for use in some other workshop. There was evidence that some firms who had been doing commercial work and who wanted their men to stay with them took up munitions in order to retain their men. It could be said that Great Britain was for the first time under the thumb of Government Departments. At the end of 1914, the percentage of unemployed was the lowest on record and the unemployment parades had ceased – at last there was work for everybody but everywhere there was a feeling of urgency.

Bell's Asbestos Factory was back working full-time by September 1914, by which time 61 of their employees were serving in the Army or the Navy. Its importance to the Navy was shown by the Government and Admiralty suspending its application of the Factory Act during the war, probably relating to hours of work, as at that time they were working both day and night, although it was not long before most factories were also working day and night. The demand for asbestos greatly increased at this time and the workforce at Bell's, which had taken over a lease of Harefield Mill, greatly expanded. It was, however, largely employed in the manufacture of war materials and had many female munitions workers, some of whom came from the mill towns from the north of England. In early 1915, in consequence of the increase in food prices due to the war, the directors decided that until further notice, the workers were to receive a temporary 'food bonus'. In mid 1916 the premises were enlarged due to the removal of the East Greenwich branch of the firm to Harefield. The factory was wholly engaged in the manufacture of millboard for the Admiralty, which was used for battleships.

Horse Shoe Bay, Harefield (Hillingdon Local History Library, Archives and Museum Service)

By the beginning of 1917 the State had gradually assumed either possession or control of railways and canals, ships and shipping, an enormous number of engineering and other works, the whole output of hay and straw etc. and in industry there was an enormous inequality of wartime demand with peacetime demand. In 1919 Government control of factories was released and normal activities were resumed.

RECRUITMENT

In the beginning, Britain's forces were composed of regular soldiers, Territorials and Volunteers. In August 1914, Britain had only a small professional army of about 150,000 men. Britain alone relied entirely on volunteers. Lord Kitchener, Secretary of War, thrice appealed for 100,000 volunteers in August and September 1914 and floods of volunteers came forward. Fathers, sons and husbands went off the war, in many cases driven by unemployment. The first recruits were ten men from Osborne, Stevens and Co, and thirty from Bell's Asbestos Works in Harefield. They were sworn in at Osborne, Stevens and Co's yard and then marched to the station for Hounslow. Before the war was six months old, more men from Britain and the British Empire were under arms than any time in history.

The Parliamentary Recruiting Committee for the Uxbridge Division was arranged in District Advisory Sub-Committees as follows: Uxbridge Urban; Uxbridge RDC (covering Hillingdon, Harefield, Cowley, West Drayton and Ickenham); Hayes Urban; Yiewsley Urban; Staines RDC (covering Harlington, Harmondsworth, Cranford, Ashford, Bedfont, Stanwell and Shepperton) and Ruislip-Northwood. The Uxbridge recruiting area covered Uxbridge Urban area -Hillingdon, Hayes, Northolt, Ickenham, Cowley and Yiewsley, but not

Harefield, and there were also Canvassing Sub-Committees.

There were numerous local men who were Reservists, former soldiers and sailors serving their 7 years' reserve commitment.

Initial enlistments were carried out by the Army's own Recruiting Service, at the depots and the regular recruiting offices, council offices (as was the case at Northwood), or at a hastily importance. It was not meant as an aid to recruitment but was ultimately used as such. In a final effort to save voluntary conscription, the Government introduced the 'Derby Scheme'. Lord Derby was appointed National Director-General of Recruiting in October 1915 resulting in more systematic recruitment.

Recruits marching through Uxbridge High Street (Hillingdon Local Studies, Archives and Museum Service)

On the basis of a National Register, every man between 18 and 41 was called up in groups as they were wanted, taking the younger single man first. However, although there had been a huge number of volunteers, this scheme was not successful and by May 1916 conscription was brought in, although men could still enlist voluntarily. Britain was by now fighting in western Europe, Turkey, the Middle East and Italy and the losses on the Somme, the bloodiest day in the history of British warfare, put the pressure on for more recruits.

Military Tribunals were set up in every Borough under the Military Service Act 1916, which were aimed at forcing unmarried men to do what they had hitherto failed to do at Lord Derby's invitation, to hear the appeals of men or local employers who could not or would not join up for reasons of occupation, religious belief, hardship or conscience. The Military Tribunals could grant temporary exemptions on condition that the applicant joined the Special Constables, VTC where they were to undertake a specified number of drills, the Motor Volunteer Corps or went to work in munitions. Most exemption claims came from employers seeking immunity for their employees on the grounds of indispensability. A large number came from men opened temporary office, such as schools and business premises.

In mid August 1914 the Uxbridge and District Emergency Committee issued an appeal in support of Lord Kitchener's second army of 100, 00 men. A few days after war was declared the first recruiting appeal posters appeared in the district. Recruiting Smoking Concerts began to be held and went on throughout hostilities. Other forms of recruitment also took place

The Territorials came into being in 1908 formed from existing volunteer units- "weekend" soldiers so vitally important at a time when the regular army had undergone such huge reductions. Territorials were only intended for home defence unless they personally volunteered to do otherwise, although by 1915 many Territorial battalions were at the Front. The proclamation calling Territorials to arms was thrown on the screen at the Uxbridge Picture Palace the evening war was declared and was received with almost a dead silence. There had been a surplus of volunteers who had sought to enlist, but the 8th Middlesex Regiment with its full complement of men along with other regiments from the regular and Territorial Army had departed for war in early September 1914. In their place one thousand West Middlesex men eagerly joined the new Territorial force, the 8th (Reserve) Battalion Middlesex Regiment. Recruiting for the Middlesex Territorial force took a very large number of men from the district as did the Royal Fusiliers. The 4/8th Middlesex (Territorial) Regiment was raised in July 1915. Notices placed in local Post Offices by the police were the usual way Reserves were recalled.

By late 1914, recruitment numbers had fallen everywhere and continuing efforts were made to recruit more men, but as the lists of those killed in action or wounded grew ever-longer, understandably there was a lot of antipathy. The National Register had started in about August 1915 and completed with certificates of registration issued by the end of the month. Every citizen aged between 16 and 65 had to supply details of age, sex and occupation and whether or not they would perform work of national engaged as market gardeners or in other forms of agriculture or those already working in munitions. Conscientious Objectors groups sprang up all over the country. In the spring of 1916, the Committee on Work of National Importance which was responsible for finding suitable work for conscientious objectors to military service wrote to the Middlesex County Council inviting them to fill vacancies on its staff with such men. The Middlesex County Council with indignant and without much discussion it was agreed that conscientious objectors should not be employed in any capacity by the County Council.

Also under Lord Derby's scheme of 1915 the basic principle for non-enlistment was that it was the State to say whether or not a man was indispensable. The various authorities interested, always with a military representative, were empowered to decide. These Tribunals, most of which were unsuccessful, were abolished in October 1918.

In a desperate attempt to recruit more soldiers a Military Service Act was passed in mid-April 1918 – hurriedly allowing the conscription of men up to the age of 51, regardless of the effect on industrial output.

By the second week of August 1914, 40-50 reservists of all classes and 10-12 Territorials had been called up and by five weeks later, in mid-September 1914 over 60 employees of Bell's Asbestos at Harefield were serving in the Army or Navy and in the first two years of war, over 100 men from the village had answered the Call of the Flag.

AIR RAIDS

A new and frightening experience was about to take place. Never before had this country experienced air raids, but the United Kingdom was attacked by Zeppelins and bombers and, near the coast, by naval bombardment. Raids by plane were more destructive than the raids by Zeppelins, the main targets of which were defined as magazines, munitions factories, ports and garrisons. The first attacks came from small floatplanes of the German Navy's first seaplane squadron. Daylight sorties were flown against Dover on 21st and 24th December 1914 followed by an attempt to reach London on Christmas Day. After the first two attacks, the RNAS concentrated resources in the Dover area. The Christmas Day raid was engaged by an RFC aircraft from Joyce Green on holiday standby. On 27th December the Admiralty introduced a larger air defence scheme for London whereby a screen of aircraft would be positioned between Grimsby and London to intercept airships flying from northern Germany and between Dungeness and London for those flying from Belgian bases. Northolt was one of the earliest aerodromes to be built in the United Kingdom.

The Commissioner of the Metropolitan Police issued letters to local Councils in May 1915 as to air-raid precautions. They advised that the public took refuge in houses so as to be out of the way of falling fragments of shells fired at enemy aircraft. All windows and doors on lower floors were to be closed, so as to prevent the admission of deleterious gas. The local Police were supplied with tripods and poles to prevent traffic from entering roads in which houses might be damaged. Another letter from the Commissioner arrived in late July 1917 informing the Council that on the approach of enemy aircraft on the way to London, sound rockets could be fired from Fire Brigade Stations in the County of London and at certain Police Stations in the Metropolitan Police District outside the County.

Although British air-raids began on German towns in September 1914, it was not until 9th January 1915 that the Kaiser approved raids on British coastal areas, docks and military establishments in the lower Thames area. Later, the Kaiser henceforth permitted the air services to attack London without restriction apart from royal palaces and historic buildings. The German Navy, unlike the German Army, was ready to start raids on the City. The first Zeppelin raid on London took place on the last day of May 1915. One unnoticed Zeppelin dropped incendiary and explosive bombs and one hand grenade on Stoke Newington, Hackney, Stepney, West Ham and Leytonstone killing six people and injuring thirty five. Unfounded rumours circulated that two Zeppelins had come down near Uxbridge.

Although local inhabitants saw nothing of the actual bombing, they could see Anti-Aircraft fire and Star Shells bursting over the capital and the neighbourhood and heard a good deal. Explosions could also be heard from miles and miles away and even the sound of guns from the distant battlefields of France and Flanders could on occasions be heard when atmospheric conditions were right. When at 3.10 am on 7th June 1917, immediately before the British infantry assault, nineteen mines charged with over a million pounds on ammonal, which lay beneath the enemy position, erupted simultaneously from Ploegsteert to Hill 60, all along the Messines ridge, the noise of the explosion of a series of the largest and deepest mines ever used in warfare, could be heard in London. Again in July 1917 the guns from Belgium could also be faintly heard.

During air-raids the Special Constabulary was always on duty occasionally for 5-6 hours at a stretch. Over 100 calls were sometimes received in the night-time.

In mid January 1915, at Harefield, in apprehension of possible air-raids precautionary measures were taken. Motors and cyclists were stopped by patrol soldiers, the car number was taken, the names of the drivers and passengers were also taken along with other information. Also by this time, lights in the shops at Harefield had been lessened.

From April, there had already been raids elsewhere, but the first raid on London took place on the night of 31st May/1st June 1915 and was carried out by the German Army Zeppelin, LZ38. Five people or so were killed and thirty five injured. At 1.20 p.m. on June 4th 1915, two of the newest naval Zeppelins left Nordholtz to attack London and the Humber area. Two sorties flew from Northolt and two from Joyce Green in defence. The RNAS were also mobilised. Although the targets had been London and the Humber area, Shoeburyness and Gravesend were bombed by mistake.

An attempted raid by three German Zeppelins (two Army and the other Naval) on London and Hull on the night of 6th/7th June 1915 caused the heaviest casualties to date in Hull where 24 people were killed. None of the Army Zeppelins reached England, but near Ghent one of these Zeppelins was bombed in the air by Flight Sub-Lieutenant Reginald A. F. J. Warneford after an hour-long chase. The craft burst into flames at about 2.30 am and fell onto a convent, killing all but one of her crew.

London itself had mainly avoided attacks until the second week in September when raids took place on two consecutive nights. The first air-raid that seriously affected London took place on the night of Wednesday 8th September 1915 when two of three

German Naval Zeppelins made landfall over the Norfolk coast. The RNAS and possibly an RFC sortie from Norwich flew against this raid. All of the twenty-six guns of the London defences were in action. The district hooter at Watford alerted residents in the north of the Borough to the raids. A few minutes later the explosion of bombs and the crackling of guns in the distance could be heard locally as bombs were dropped on Golders Green followed by more along a line from Euston to Liverpool Street. Many local people journeying in and around London saw the enemy craft and the bombs dropping. The Fire Brigade, VDF and local special constables were called out for both of these raids.

A Zeppelin raid took place in the night of 13th/14th October 1915. Five naval airships, the L.11, L.13, L.14, L.15 and L.16 set out for the attack from Nordholtz shortly after noon. There seems to have been a very distinct tactical plan for this raid, which was carried out in proper squadron formation. The L13, captained by Mathy the leader of the formation, swept round by St. Albans, but altered his course over Rickmansworth immediately after he had seen L.15 under fire, and headed south over the course of the river Colne, passing over on its way to Staines, and Guildford before making its way home, but not before dropping incendiary missiles at Woolwich. This raid was one of the deadliest of the war. 71 people were killed - 38 alone were killed in London and a number of soldiers in camp at Hertford also lost their lives, 128 people were injured and damage was estimated at over £80,000. The raids ceased with the onset of winter.

The longest airship raid took place in East Anglia on the night of 2nd/3rd September 1916 when 16 Army and Navy Zeppelins airships attacked between the Humber and Ipswich. With the German army and navy combining for the first, and last, time to attack, this was the biggest airship raid of the war (it was also, for the Germans, an utter failure). It was to be the only time during the war that Army airships bombed the same target simultaneously. One airship, the SL II, commanded by Hauptmann Wilhelm Schramm, reached London, the place of his birth. Lt. William Leefe-Robinson from 39 Squadron, who had received some training at Northolt, although stationed at Sutton's Farm at the time, won his VC on 2nd September 1916 for shooting down the Zeppelin, SL II at Cuffley, near Potter's Bar, in Hertfordshire. The flash of the exploding SL II could be seen over a radius of some 40 to 50 miles and despite the time being 02.25am it was seen by hundreds of thousands of cheering people. It was very clearly seen by the local men on duty and as some of the local trains were so late many inhabitants were able to see the spectacle themselves. Others were woken from their slumber by the sound of Anti-Aircraft fire and fled into the streets half-dressed as they had done before in moonlight raids and also were to do in later attacks. The news that an air attack was impending had spread all over London. The hospitals were ready for any emergency, fire stations were prepared to respond to any call, every Special Constable had been called up, at every Police station surgeons and nurses had come on duty as had ambulance men with stretchers at the ready. Every vantage spot was crowded with spectators as dozens of beams from the searchlights showed from every part of London and the outer sections. London had never seen such brilliant illumination.

Two Zeppelin airships were also brought down in or near Potter's Bar in September 1916 and the 35 members of the two crews were buried with military honours in the churchyard and their names commemorated on stone tablets set into the wall of the church. Of the two German Army airships which raided on the night of September 7th 1916, one struck Millwall, Deptford, Greenwich and Woolwich docks. The other dropped bombs on greenhouses at Cheshunt and later found herself over London. It was the first Army airship to reach London and the penultimate Army airship to appear in the London area for the rest of the war. Not to be outdone by its rival service, four German Naval airships raided England the very next day. One, the L. 13, commanded by Heinrich Mathy, without a doubt the greatest airship commander of the war, admired by both friend and foe alike, reached London where some bombs were dropped.

A further raid to place at the end of September. The districts attacked during the night and in the early hours of the morning were the South Coast, East Coast, North East Coast and North Midlands. Seven airships took part in this raid which killed 36 people. Two Zeppelins, L.32 and L.33, both of recent construction, were brought down in Essex. The first airship was destroyed by an aeroplane, having evaded gunfire. The second airship was hit by gunfire from the London Defences.

The last Zeppelin raid of the year on London was on the night of October 1st/2nd 1916 when eleven Zeppelins left their sheds heading for the Midlands and north-east England. However Commander

Mathy headed his L.31 towards London. He came in by way of Lowestoft and after extensive meanderings over Hertfordshire, came as far south as Cheshunt where he released most of his bombs (30 high explosive and 26 incendiary) and set off westwards. Although he had managed to avoid the ground defences, he was brought down by Second Lieutenant W.J. Tempest an RFC pilot from No. 39 Squadron (North Weald) who had been patrolling between Joyce Green and Hainault. The wreckage came down in a field outside Potters Bar. Mathy and all his crew were dead. For a while, the Midlands and the north-east of England still suffered attacks. The successes around London led to the formation of more Home Defence Squadrons.

A daylight raid took place on 28th November 1916 when one lone LVG.CIV aircraft had London as its target. It flew at a great height, taking advantage of a slight haze which hung over the city which it approached over Croydon and Mitcham. The aircraft was unobserved until its bombs began to fall injuring nine people. Again No. 39 Squadron were in action with other squadrons and the RNAS, amounting to 21 sorties. In broad daylight the aircraft dropped six 22lb. bombs between the Brompton Road and Victoria Station. By the time the Home Defence Wing had ordered any RFC patrols at 12.45 hours, the aircraft was almost at the Sussex coast and none of the defenders saw anything. Four planes from 39 Squadron left North Weald, Hounslow, Suttons Farm and Hainault at just after 13.00 hours. At 14.15 hours it was brought down by the French when its engine failed at Dunkirk and the crew, two naval lieutenants, captured. With them was a large-scale map of London.

Between 1914 and the end of 1916 there had been 43 airship and 28 aeroplane attacks all over England.

The German Gotha bomber aeroplane had been flight-tested in the autumn of 1916 and 30 were ready for action by February 1917. Uxbridge 'Specials' and VTC were called out again for an air-raid in the late afternoon of 25th May 1917 when 22 of the German's new huge Gotha aeroplanes were sighted heading for Essex, the target again being London. The raiders made for the Thames and then swerved south-east away from London and headed for Kent. Several bombs were dropped on an airfield near Folkestone and the neighbouring town of Shornecliffe was bombed as was Shornecliffe Camp, causing 100 Canadian casualties.

A daylight raid on 5th June 1917, which left 13 killed and 34 injured, had Sheerness as its target. Again the RFC and RNAS pilots were sent up - 62 sorties were made. No. 35 (T) Squadron took off from Northolt in new Bristol Fighters aircraft, in pursuit of 22 Gothas. This is the first recorded flight from Northolt. Although the RFC and RNAS had no success, Anti-Aircraft guns situated on either side of the Thames Estuary did. Gotha 660, piloted by Vizefeldwebel Erich Kluck, commanded by Leutnant H. Franke with Unteroffizier Georg Schumacher the gunner crashed into the water. Only Schumacher survived.

On June 13th 1917, of the 18 Gotha bombers which had taken off from St. Denis Westrem and Gontrode during the morning, one aircraft had become detached and headed for Margate whilst over Foulness three more peeled off and made for the Thames Estuary area. The remaining 14 large aircraft flew in diamond formation and approached London from the north-west. One pilot of the RNAS had been able to bring his guns to bear on an enemy machine but had to break off when his Lewis gun jammed. The RFC were more successful and several pilots made contact with the enemy. On this occasion no German aircraft was shot down but 162 civilians in London, including 18 schoolchildren from the Upper North Street School who were sheltering in a cellar where the bomb fell, were killed. 432 were injured, including several people slightly injured at Headstone near Harrow, wounded by falling glass and masonry. In all, almost as many as the casualties of all the Zeppelin raids of 1915 and damage amounted to almost £130,000. A public outcry saw the immediate improvement in anti-aircraft defences. From September of that year the Gotha aeroplanes were forced to attack at night.

The targets in the daylight raid of 4th July 1917 were Harwich and Felixstowe. In the early hours of the morning 25 Gothas were despatched. It was at the naval air station at Felixstowe, the main objective of the raid, that 17 men were killed, mostly naval ratings. It was in this incident that David Rogers from Harefield, a 19 year old Officer's Steward with the RNAS was severely injured. He died on 6th July 1917 at Shatley Hospital and his body brought back to Harefield for burial.

24 Gothas were despatched for a heavy daylight raid on London on 7th July 1917, which killed 57 and injured 193 people. Almost 100 British fighters and all guns attacked them shooting down five.

After the air-raids of mid 1917, hundreds of air-raid refugees from London arrived in the district.

Ramsgate and Dover were the targets for the 22nd August 1917 daylight raid by 15 Gothas. Guns based at Harrow and Hanwell, amongst others, were engaged.

Another raid occurred at about on 24th September 1917 when Navy Zeppelins targeted the Midlands and northeast. Star Shells bursting in the air and lighting up the enemy's position could plainly be seen in the district. The noise was awesome. Take-cover notices were evident in all the local villages. After this raid, huge rents were asked for locally.

These large Gotha aeroplanes also set out to bomb London, night after night from 28th September to 2nd October. They became known as the 'harvest moon raids'. Londoners had never heard such a bombardment as the raid which took place on 28th September and in the brilliant moonlight the barrage from north-west London was clearly visible.

By now, the increased density of the guns and lights around London had forced the Germans to fly even larger formations of airships – at night. From late September 1917 a small number of huge Riesen aircraft- the largest used in either war – began to accompany the Gotha aircraft. The raid on the night of 19th/20th October 1917 took place with a raging gale at very high altitudes above calm. The target was northern England but the raiders were blown off course by the strong winds and some crossed London. Because of the mist the guns kept silent. The acoustic conditions muffled the noise of their engines and guns and became known as 'the Silent Raid'. Out of the 11 Zeppelins that set out, only 6 returned home - four airships were lost over France and one crashed on London. It was the biggest Zeppelin disaster to the Germans of the whole war so far. Both L55 and L45 passed the western outskirts of London. Most of L45's bombs fell to the north-west of London. Some big bombs were dropped near Harrow from L45 as it sailed over London, dropping more bombs on Piccadilly and Camberwell before heading for France, leaving 33 people killed and 50 injured. The force of the exploding bombs dropped near Harrow was plainly felt locally. From now on, the Zeppelins mostly confined themselves to attacking British submarines in the North Sea. There had been 208 Zeppelin flights with 522 people killed.

Following an interval of some six weeks or so the area once again heard gunfire. On the night of 29th/30th January 1918 a number of attacks were carried out by hostile aeroplanes between 10pm and 12.30am. About 15 enemy planes, coming in small detachments, crossed the coast and four Giant aircraft headed for London. It was about 8 in the evening when the warning of maroons was fired followed an hour later by the first guns. Most people made promptly for shelter but many continued in the streets until the guns were heard. Two machines reached London where one was viciously attacked near Tottenham and then headed for home, but not before dropping some bombs near Wanstead.   Another aeroplane was attacked on its inward path, turned at Hertford and headed for Brentford where it dropped some bombs on Whitestile Road killing the wife of Sgt Major Curley who was serving with the Colours, their five children, a niece and an invalid lady who resided with the family and two men at the Water Works before making for the Chiswick area where more bombs were dropped. A salvo of guns in the neighbourhood proved the end of the raid. Another raid took place the following night. Public indignation had by now reached seething point.

London was the primary target for the night raid that took place on 16th/17th February 1918 and the local area was more than usually within the sound of the guns. Five German Giant aircraft had been dispatched and the Mercedes-engined Giants attacked Dover.

When on the night of 19th/20th May 1918 over 40 German heavy bombers took off to bomb London, the sound of guns was fairly distinct locally. However, the flashes and rumbles of the aerial display were more impressive. During this raid, Hayes Fire Brigade was on duty for 3½ hours. The last raid, a Zeppelin attack on the Midlands, took place on the night of 5/6th August 1918. Balloons had been inflated and released from Uxbridge for night observation twice in this week.

Almost every part of London, apart from the west and south-west had been attacked. Between December 24th 1914 and June 17th 1918 there had been 51 airship raids and 57 aeroplane raids all over the country. A total number of 8,578 bombs had been dropped and by the end of the War, the total number of British air raid casualties amounted to 1,414 dead, 3,416 injured and material damage amounting to almost £3, 000,000. London suffered more than half of the casualties – 670 killed and 1,962 injured.

During night raids factories ceased production until the all clear was sounded and all trains, apart from those underground, were stopped.

To begin with there were no air-raid shelters and air-raid warnings were unheard of. The Lights (London) Order placed restrictions on the lighting of London and 10 miles around after dark from the beginning of the war but this did not cover this area, so local Councils made their own arrangements. In late June 1915 councils received letters from the Metropolitan Police pointing out the advisability of extinguishing all street lights in the event of an air-raid. Gradually houses, factories, railways and trams were all brought under regulations tending to increase darkness. By the winter of 1916 every house and shop had its windows carefully shaded with dark curtains and the street lamps had been reduced in number and obscured so as to give no more than a glimmer of light and the headlights of vehicles were reduced in power.

Church services were confined to daylight hours, as were theatres, restaurants and cinemas. The kerbs of many London streets were whitewashed so they could be visible to vehicles and pedestrians. People were also prosecuted for failing to have red lights on their cars.

Local public clocks, in common with other timepieces throughout the country including Big Ben, had all been stopped in the early days of the air-raids. Most of these were not to come on again until mid 1919.

HOUSING

The war put an end to residential building and the growth of outer London ceased. Plans to extend the Breakspear Institute were put on hold and in mid August 1914 Harefield Parish Council asked Uxbridge Rural District Council to do all in their power to commence building the much needed houses at Harefield to provide accommodation for the workers and employment for those out of work.

Large premises were taken over for various purposes. Harefield House was taken over as a hospital. Everywhere there was a shortage of houses and rooms in houses. Rooms in houses were used to billet soldiers, although there was a regulation that soldiers would not be billeted in the house of the wife of a soldier serving abroad. For instance, in mid August 1914 soldiers were billeted at and around Uxbridge as part of the general scheme for the outer defence of London. The billeting of soldiers became law and many prosecutions took place. Refugees from Belgium streamed into England after September 1914 and workers working in the local factories after they turned over to making munitions also had to be housed. Everywhere there was a shortage of houses and rooms in houses.

Rickmansworth Road, Harefield (Hillingdon Local Studies, Archives and Museum Service)

Landlords within a 10 mile radius of London were given an allowance to help with rent, but this did not apply to any part of Harefield and bad feeling was rife. There were heated debates concerning what some thought was their loss of 3s 6d. Rents rose significantly in 1915 with the influx of many people and were soon controlled by law and put back to pre-war costs so that extortionate rents could not be asked. The influx of Belgian refugees and serving men as well as houses taken over as hospitals, all aggravated the serious housing shortage everywhere and after the first of the Zeppelin raids on this country when air-raid refugees fled the capital, the demand for accommodation outside the capital became urgent. Following the autumn 1917 raids there was further demand for apartments in this district and fabulous prices were being offered. However, a large number of people, especially women with children, coming to the district from London to escape air-raids could not find sleeping accommodation and walked the streets at night. During the raids even at Harefield enquiries were made for rooms.

Munitions workers who flooded to factories in Harefield and Watford from almost anywhere, especially after the autumn of 1915 after the munitions factories had been constructed (2 at Watford), preferred to lodge with families. Housing was at a premium.

Two blocks of sleeping cubicles and a canteen were approved at a Council meeting in the spring of 1917. The canteen for 800 people erected for the benefit of the employees at Bell's Asbestos Works at Harefield was due to be opened on 25th February 1918 but this did not take place as planned because of the difficulty of obtaining supplies. The planned hostel on completion was to be used to relieve the housing difficulties at Harefield. In early September 1918 both the canteen and hostel for

34

feeding and sleeping accommodation for the large number of local women munitions workers opened.

In the autumn of 1917 the Council (Uxbridge Rural District Council) wrote to the Local Government Board pointing out that 75 extra houses were desperately needed in Harefield. A site had been identified on Poors Lane on which to construct 50 workmen's dwellings. The Board's standard reply was that they were in no position to sanction any loan for housing. Towards the end of the war, dilapidated houses in the High Street which were owned by the Co-operative Society and which had been used to house people, were ordered by the Council to be pulled down.

With the influx of so many people, the Government encouraged local authorities to provide more housing, although up to this time it was the popular belief that private builders would continue to provide all normal housing needs. This, however, had proved impossible and with the lack of house building, serious problems were encountered after the war.

SCHOOLS

The 1902 Education Act provided for the establishment of education other than elementary. Up until this time most of the secondary schools had been private. The War put a stop to the flow of educational progress and after the war the country's financial difficulties permitted few improvements.

Schooling suffered many interruptions, from staff joining up, illnesses, female staff having time off when their husbands came home from leave etc. From almost the start of the war, Belgian refugee children attended local schools and the adults were given lessons in English. Air-raid refugees were also housed locally and it is known that their children were admitted to Ickenham National School in October 1917 and another 10 in late February 1918. Some also finished their education at Uxbridge County School. Local authorities were under intense pressure to suspend the school attendance by-laws so that children could be released to undertake 'national work' and there was also a marked increase in early school-leaving to go to work. Summer holidays were mostly changed from August to July so that schoolchildren could help with the harvest.

In the spring of 1915, the Chairman of the Education Committee authorised pupils over the age of 13 to be excused (not legally exempt from school attendance) from attending at school for the purpose of agricultural or Government work on the following conditions:-

1. The child was over the age of 13
2. The wages were satisfactory
3. Any child excused must return to school of they give up this work before he or she reaches the age of 14

In the spring of 1918 the Education Committee informed all schools that it was not advisable to grant further exemption for work on the land to children between 13 and 14 'because of the evil results which follow'.

In the spring of 1915 a circular was issued by the Middlesex Education Committee advising schools in the county to immediately prepare a plan of action in the case of air-raids. It was advised that in the event of a raid the children should carry on working but be as far away as possible from the windows. They would not be released from the school until it had been ascertained that all danger had passed. The Committee also advised a strongly worded letter be sent to all parents informing them that they would be unable to collect their children at such a time. Each school differed in its drilling arrangements. In some when a whistle was blown the children had to lie flat on their stomachs; in others children were told to get under a desk. The Police were asked to give as long a notice as possible to schools in the event of an impending air-raid. New air-raid instructions, dated 23rd July 1917, were sent to all schools, which cancelled air-raid drills in force and advised them of the drilling of school children in preparation of air-raids. Children living in roads close to the school were to be sent home and children who were living in roads too far from the school were to remain in the school and remain sheltered in the basement, unless written instructions to the contrary were received from their parents or guardians.

Most school children saved money that was collected for war savings and also contributed most willingly to fund raising and making 'comforts' for the troops – although not everything was appreciated by the Tommies.

For schools the difficulty of the war years was mainly a matter of staffing and towards the end of 1915 the headmasters of schools with an average attendance of no more than 350 were encouraged to take a class. In early 1916 it was reported that out of a total of well over 200 teachers in Middlesex County elementary schools, only 10 had not joined the Colours or attested under the Derby scheme and in the secondary schools, out of 229 teachers, over 200 had enlisted or attested.

HAREFIELD, THE MEMORIAL.   Coles, Photographer, Watford.

Harefield 'The Memorial' c1911 (Hillingdon Local Studies, Archives and Museum Service)

By May 1918 more than 22,000 teachers had left the schools for the Colours, after a further call was made on the teaching profession made by the Board of Education and the National Service Ministry. A few men under 25 and a rather larger number under 32 had been kept in the schools by local education authorities as being indispensable. These were now to be called up and a serious situation was expected in the schools. The Middlesex Education Committee requested that in the *'present crisis the staffing of the Schools should be on the basis of the actual Code requirements wherever possible and the Committee would be glad if the Managers could see their way to release one of their teachers to assist in other schools if necessary'.*

Head teachers often gave news of teachers and pupils and were very sad when they had to report the deaths on active service of former pupils or staff. In late August 1914 Mr. W.J. Jeffrey, headmaster of the Council School at Harefield opened the school after the holidays in his Territorial uniform. Almost immediately he went back to join the company of Territorials he was connected with in north London and acted as an ammunition carrier in the fighting of early 1915. The school caretaker, Mr. Hastings, an old Reservist, was also called up. At a recruiting meeting on behalf of the 1/8th Middlesex Regiment, held at the Memorial Hall before the war, he was the only one to enlist. He, by now in the King's Royal Rifle Corps, was severely wounded in the thigh and shoulder by shrapnel at the Front in September 1915 and brought back to England to be treated in hospital in Leicester. David Rogers, a former pupil, who was with the RNAS at Felixstowe was badly wounded during an air-raid on the east coast on 4th July 1917 and died two days later. William Batchelor, who had been awarded the Military Medal, was a father of three. He was killed in action on 3rd March 1918. He had enlisted at Towcester, Northamptonshire, in November 1915 and served in the Royal West Surreys with the Expeditionary Force from 17th September 1915. Frank Ryder was born at Harefield on 11th March 1898, son of James and Emma Ryder of Riverside Cottage, Harefield. He enlisted in the Middlesex Regiment in August 1916 and later transferred to the 8th East Surrey Regiment. He died from wounds received on 8th January 1918, when he was taken prisoner in Belgium. Charles Watkins who worked on his father's farm at West Hyde died of wounds in France on 31st May 1918, aged 22. He served with the Royal Horse and Field Artillery and had been in the firing line. He was taken unconscious to a Canadian hospital on the 31st and died later the same day. However, some very good tidings in the midst of gloom were heartening. William Crook serving with the 1st Border Regiment was awarded the Military medal in early 1918 for carrying wounded under shell fire. In September 1916, Robert Ryder, a former labourer, the son of Robert, was awarded the Victoria Cross for bravery in the capture of Thiepval. He was serving in 'B' Coy, 12th Middlesex Regiment. Mr. Arthur Paget Cole, a good pianist, who had been educated at Uxbridge County School, where he had been their first Senior Prefect, and was one of the assistant masters at the Council school, returned to his duties in early 1919. He had for two years served as Lieutenant with the London Rifle Brigade and had been wounded in the first onslaught of the Germans in spring offensive of March 1918. He had at first been stationed at Exeter before going to the Front.

LEISURE PURSUITS

Within the first weeks of war, over 1,000 local footballers who were registered with the Middlesex County Football Association had joined the colours and this figure increased day by day. As young men joined up, many clubs were forced to close through lack of members. This resulted in land becoming earmarked, whilst other sports grounds had already been built upon. The MCFA cancelled all their coming season competitions and urged able-bodied men to join up without delay. As leagues and clubs disbanded local sides found opposition from various army units that were stationed nearby at

Denham or Slough. All teams were encouraged to play matches to raise funds for war relief. The Uxbridge Football Club had already lost its ground at Hillingdon House to the Royal Flying Corps and was loaned a field at Cowley. The Great Western Suburban League suspended all football fixtures for the 1914-1915 season when ten clubs dropped out – Uxbridge and Southall were the only ones remaining. The Uxbridge and District League had already been disbanded. Early in 1916 Uxbridge FC became one of the last of the local clubs to stop playing. It appears that professional football was stopped in July 1915 and replaced with regional leagues where players, who would only play on Saturdays, were unpaid, although the Brentford Football Club was still in existence in August 1917 and were welcoming offers of assistance from players stationed at military camps or munition works who would play for them wearing the Brentford colours. A London Works League and a Munitions League were formed for the employees of factories engaged in the war effort. Football matches were arranged between women working at local munitions factories and were held in aid of Red Cross funds.

The Middlesex County Football Association had hoped that cup matches would be run in the latter half of the 1918-1919 season, but this was impossible with so few clubs being in a position to resume playing.

Cricket carried on in a desultory fashion for a time, although Harefield Cricket Club had cancelled all its fixtures by early September 1914. By late August 1914 Uxbridge and West Middlesex Athletic Club had lost 25% of its total membership. As its membership further gradually declined as every member of military age enlisted, in September 1914 they offered their premises for the accommodation of refugees through Lady Hillingdon.

It took a number of years for sports clubs to recover from the war, in which some fine local players were killed in action. After the war ended, clubs made hard efforts and gradually clubs reformed, albeit sometimes years later, and were successful in reviving the pre-war activities.

HOSPITALS

The flow of casualties from the various theatres of war soon overwhelmed the existing medical facilities in the United Kingdom. The War Office had military hospitals erected in favourable districts, towns set aside parts of their infirmaries for the wounded and in some cases built hospitals and handed them over fully equipped to the military

 authorities. Many wealthy people converted their residences into hospitals and bore sole charge and others handed their houses over to the Red Cross Society, or to be used as hospitals or places of convalescence.

Inside a hospital train

(H.W. Wilson, The Great War)

On the outbreak of War, Southampton became the No. I Military Embarkation Port, and the port of departure for the British Expeditionary Force, as all railway lines led directly or indirectly to it. The first convoy of 111 sick and wounded men arrived here on 24th August 1914 and were taken in the War Department Ambulance Train to the Royal Victoria Hospital, Netley. The new Marine station at Dover, which had not yet been completed, was ready on 2nd January 1915 to receive up to two hospital ships and six ambulance trains at the same time. It had been a rush job to finish the Marine station. The stream of wounded from Flanders seemed never-ending and finally it was decided to complete the station within a week. Work started on 23rd December and by working day and night right through Christmas, the work was finished to schedule.

There were 4 ambulance trains in service in 1914. By July 1916 there were 28. Over 75 hospital ships were in service during the war. In the end the total number of sick and wounded British and Commonwealth servicemen from all theatres of war conveyed in ambulance trains from British ports up to April 1919 was 2,680,000, divided fairly equally between Southampton and Dover, apart from a small number landed at other ports. The vast majority of those arriving at Southampton and Dover were the wounded from France. Those from various Eastern campaigns were landed at Avonmouth, Devonport or Liverpool.

There were almost 200 railway stations in Britain which received convoys of the sick and wounded. Denham and Southall, on the Great Western Railway, were the nearest stations to this area which received military ambulance trains which had been sent from either Dover, the principal port for the transport of the wounded, or from Southampton, or from both.

Harefield had a complement of 26 medical officers and 112 other ranks, 26 sisters, 36 staff nurses, 120 Australian VAD nurses seconded from British hospitals and 6 masseuses. Many local people also volunteered to help. Eleven NCOs and men of the Australian Medical Transport Corps, seven ambulances, two touring cars, one motor lorry and one motorcycle carried out evacuation from Denham Station. Mr. Randall Palmer, licensee of the Cricketer's Arms was one of those who drove a motor-bus between the hospital and Denham Station. The speed that some of these vehicles travelled at was far too fast and complaints were made. By 1917 the road between the hospital and Denham was in a deplorable state of disrepair.

The distribution of patients after their arrival in this country was complicated. Their destination depended very largely on the nature of their disability. It was essential that certain cases should go to hospitals specialising in particular types of treatment. For instance, the chief place for face wounds was the Cambridge Hospital, Aldershot until 1917 when a new hospital for face injuries opened at Frognal near Sidcup in Kent. To begin with casualties returning to Britain would receive initial treatment in British hospitals, and would be transferred to convalescent hospitals to make way for new arrivals from the front. In many cases these were in large houses lent by their owners. Australian, New Zealand and Canadian casualties usually went to hospitals which their own medical personnel had established in Britain. South Africans were nursed at a military hospital at Richmond. Similarly Jewish servicemen were usually sent to the Beech House Military Hospital Brondesbury, London or the Mote Auxiliary Hospital, Maidstone, the two main hospitals that looked after that particular faith until the Tudor House Military Hospital at Hampstead Heath (which was the only hospital intended exclusively for the use of Jewish soldiers) opened in October 1918. It received a large number of patients until the middle of 1919.

To facilitate distribution, advanced information was cabled about the various categories of patients (lying and sitting patients) on each hospital ship and the estimated time of arrival. These categories were subdivided into the numbers of officers, nurses and other ranks, with further subdivisions into surgical, medical, infectious, mental, and any other special cases. Patients were labelled with one of the five areas corresponding to their home area – London and Southern, West of England, Midlands, North England and Scotland and Ireland. This meant there was a possibility that patients would be sent to a hospital close to where they lived. The area home commands showing the bed situation in their larger and specialist hospitalssent daily notification.

At the beginning of the War Australian casualties had been admitted to British hospitals but as the War progressed it became obvious that Australian hospitals were necessary and by October 1916 three auxiliary hospitals had been established. The first hospital - No. 1 Australian Auxiliary Hospital was in Harefield and was opened in 1915. This was followed by the second at Southall, at a large school built in 1858 to educate the poor children of the Parish of St. Marylebone, which held as many as 800 Australian patients and staff, and which eventually specialised in the fitting of artificial limbs. The third was at Dartford. Smaller hospitals were also established at Welwyn where there were 24 beds and at Moreton Gardens, Kensington with 40 beds.

Harefield Park (Hillingdon Local Studies, Archives and Museum Service)

Harefield Park and its estate of 250 acres was owned by a wealthy Australian from New South Wales - Mr. Charles Billyard-Leake and his wife, Letitia, (their son, Second Lieutenant C.R. Billyard-Leake serving with the Rifle Brigade, was awarded the Military Cross in 1918) who offered it to the Australian Ministry of Defence as a convalescent home where officers, warrant officers, NCOs and men of the A.I.F. would recuperate after illness or injury. It was also to act as a depot for collecting invalids for return to Australia. The property was on three storeys with outbuildings, lakes, shrubberies, flower gardens, paddocks in some 250 acres. This offer was accepted in December 1914, and within a month the Australian MOD had approved staff - one captain, one sergeant, one corporal, four men as wardsmen and orderlies, one matron and five nursing sisters. Ethel Gray, an Australian Queen Alexandra Nurse from Melbourne was specifically selected for the job and proceeded to England, with five nurses, arriving on 26[h] March 1915. She found the house still containing much of the original furniture and carpets, which had to be removed. The Billyard-Leakes moved into Black Jack's Mill.

Ambulance men lined up at a station waiting to disembark the wounded (H.W. Wilson. The Great War)

Originally it was estimated that the house would accommodate 50 soldiers in winter and 150 during the spring-summer. Hutted wards would have to be built on the front lawn. Ethel Gray had almost six weeks to get everything ready. By May, 80 beds were ready. The first commanding officer and five orderlies who were sailing on the troopship '*Runic*' were due mid May. In May 1915 arrangements were being made to extend the accommodation to 500 beds. Australian and New Zealand troops who had mostly fought at Gallipoli were expected. The first patients (7 of them) arrived via Lemnos and Malta on 2nd June 1915. On 17th June more wounded arrived. This made a total of 80 patients. Huts were put up all over the place - most where the cricket pitches had been. A mortuary was situated beyond the kitchen garden. By 22nd June the hospital had 170 patients, two weeks later there were 362. The Harefield Asbestos Works offered to convert a bay windowed room into an operating theatre and on 9th July the first operation was carried out.

The 'ANZAC Hospital' (Hillingdon Local Studies, Archives and Museum Service)

In the first week of January 1916 the first patients were evacuated to Australia. The first death occurred just over one month later when on 8th February 1916 Robert Sidney Wake, 5th Battalion Australian Infantry, who was born at Cullercoats, Northumberland, died of wounds. He was in his early 20s and was buried at St. Mary's Church, Harefield, as are all that died here.

At first the practice was that wounded Australians on their arrival in England would proceed to one or other of the many British General Military

48

Hospitals and when well enough they would be transferred to Harefield. It was soon realised that with the enormity of casualties, it should become a fully equipped hospital. In mid to late May 1916, the number of patient dropped to about 100, but quickly rose to 500 as a result of the men wounded in France. By now, there was accommodation at the hospital for about 960 casualties. By October 1916 it became a hospital - the Australian Auxiliary Hospital No. I - with increased medical and nursing personnel. An artificial limb workshop opened in December 1915 and an eye, ear and throat ward in January 1916. At the end of 1916 Ethel Gray was posted to France and was succeeded by Matron Gould who in turn was replaced by Miss Ross in November 1917.

The 'ANZAC Hospital' (Hillingdon Local Studies, Archives and Museum Service)

It gradually developed into a specialist centre for radiography and electrotherapeutic services, with 43 wards. By the end of the War accommodation had increased to 1,000 beds by the erection of further huts and other types of speciality treatment had evolved for eye, ear, and nose and throat conditions.

When the hospital opened supplies of food were arranged through the Army Service Corps (ASC) at Hounslow. In November 1915 a committee was formed to purchase all foods on the open market. Colletts General Stores at Harefield supplied the bread. The produce of the farm, usually despatched to London, was also used for supplying the hospital. Tenders were invited for the supply of fresh milk, which by mid 1917 had grown to 143 gallons every four months. In early 1918 an acre was given over to grow foodstuffs as part of the allotment scheme. The main kitchen situated in the house, was relieved by a field kitchen in the grounds constructed before mid 1915. Strangely enough Edwin Dancer, a greengrocer of Harefield, also kept a large number of chickens, which, from May 1916, he gave to the Northwood War Hospital.

The King and Queen, attended by the Countess of Minto and Captain B. Godfrey-Faussett, RN, visited the 1st Australian Auxiliary Hospital on 16th August 1915 for two hours, and in the same month a sentry box was placed at the entrance. The Australian Prime Minister also visited the hospital as did other leading Australians. In the Spring of 1917, the Duke of Connaught presented several medals for gallant service in France and Gallipoli.

The 'Long Ramp' was the main thoroughfare. It was an open board walk which started under a big oak tree and joined to other covered ways. It was busy most days with men arriving or departing and also gave good protection in the winter months.

The casualties wore a light blue uniform with a red tie whilst in hospital, but once they were well enough to venture outside they also wore a blue band on their arm. Londoners called this 'the blue badge of courage'. Their boots and shoes were repaired by Harefield saddler, Mr. Gough.

Ambulance outside the Hospital (Hillingdon Local Studies, Archives and Museum Service)

A great deal of thought went into the providing recreational facilities for them. For instance, Harefield Park Boomerang was the magazine of the No. 1 Australian Auxiliary Hospital, Harefield, which was started in December 1916 by Pte. C.A.Evenden and Pte. H.J. Kemp and afterwards controlled by a committee. In 1917 a band was organised. Patients undertook fancy work which was exhibited and sports days were also held. A patients' canteen was opened and put under the control of the Director of recreation and study and an Orderlies Canteen opened for all ranks below Sergeant.

By early 1918, the canteen had made healthy profits and these were used to decorate the Recreation Hall. A large stove was also provided and two pianos. The Breakspear Institute, which had a very small extension built in late 1915, was also greatly used by the wounded Australians. The director of recreation and study had been before a medical board and passed for field service at home only, although three times his case had come before the Military Tribunal, which in June 1916 gave conditional exemption. Many invitations for outings were extended to the wounded men, but the shortage of transport was a problem, especially in November 1917 when there were as many as 1,100 patients being treated in the hospital. Fortunately many of the locals rallied round to help.

ANZAC Hospital (Hillingdon Local Studies, Archives and Museum Service)

There were no reports of antisocial behaviour on the part of the Australians at Harefield, apart from very occasionally, unlike the wounded and recuperating Australian soldiers and some staff from the temporary military hospital situated at Southall who had been banned from Southall park for most of the war because of their bad behaviour, and very late in the war were also banned from all the public houses in Southall, although it had been made illegal to sell intoxicants to a member of His Majesty's Forces who was undergoing hospital treatment. However, local boys were discovered smuggling alcoholic drinks into the hospital and were severely dealt with.

In 1916, Private J. Naughton 3rd Battalion 'D' Coy Australian Expeditionary Force, a badly wounded patient wrote, under the title of 'My Short Career', a short record of his service – 'I enlisted August 26th 1914, left Australia on October 19th 1914, landed in Egypt on December 3rd 1914, left Egypt on April 2nd 1915, for the Dardanelles, landed Gallipoli Peninsula on April 25th 1915, wounded at Lone Pine on August 14th 1915 – result both hands blown off and badly wounded in right leg'. It was a perfectly legible account, written with a pen secured between his wrists.

Front and back pages from 'The Boomerang' (Hillingdon Local Studies, Archives and Museum Service)

An incident which caused much sadness to the patients was when Jimmy the kangaroo, the hospital mascot, was shot dead in May 1918 by a local farmer who had no idea what sort of animal it was. Jimmy had been presented to one of the volunteer workers in October 1916 by the daughter of Sir William Birdwood, General Officer Commanding the ANZACs. It was Sir William himself who had first thought of the word ANZAC when asked to supply a handy telegraphic address in 1915. Another mascot, a cockatoo, would imitate the sound of a 'Turkish shell'.

The 'ANZAC Hospital' (Hillingdon Local Studies, Archives and Museum Service)

Reveille was at 6am. Fall In was heard at 6.15am followed by half an hour of exercises followed by breakfast. Sick Parade and lectures took place in the morning and after dinner a march or some other exercise was obligatory which lasted until 4pm. After tea the rest of the day was free. First Post was at 9. 30pm, Last Post 10.00pm and Lights Out half an hour later.

The hospital was open to visitors on Wednesday, Saturday and Sunday between 2pm and 5.30pm.

The hospital did not treat officers, instead they were cared for at 1 Moreton Gardens, The Boltons, Kensington, remaining a Casualty Clearing Depot throughout the war. At Harefield, altogether over fifty buildings were erected, forty-three of which were used for the reception of patients. In 1916 when the house was full, Mr. Billyard-Leake offered for rent the 'Red House by the Strolleys' in Park Lane opposite the Officers' Mess.

Thousands of wounded Australian soldiers passed through, one source estimates 49,000 wounded Australians passed through the hospital, but it maybe as many as 100,000 and in nine months in 1917 there were 10,232 admissions. The largest number of patients at any one time was 970. 111 soldiers died, including at least one suicide, and one nursing sister, Ruby Dickinson from Sydney, died of influenza in the Sisters' hospital in the afternoon of 23rd June 1918. She had been at Harefield since January 1918, having previously been nursing in a number of hospitals in France. A Union Jack was borrowed from Harefield Council School to cover the coffins of those that died at the hospital and it was lent for the duration of the War. Early in 1917 a fund was started for the erection of headstones to all the graves.

In January 1919, 72 patients were admitted and 691 discharged. At the same time Woodlands, which had been taken over in March 1918 after standing empty for some time, and Cranfield House, Harefield, which had been the quarters of the Women's VAD at the hospital were vacated. When the institution closed the remaining patients were transferred to Weymouth.

Immediately after the war Harefield Park house was purchased by the Council and became a TB sanatorium in 1921. It was considered to be the finest and most up-to-date sanatorium in England. The north wards were constructed during World War Two for use by the Emergency Medical Services. It later became part of the world-renowned Harefield Hospital.

RATIONING and the CULTIVATION OF LAND ORDER 1916

During 1915, almost a quarter of British ships had been requisitioned. With this shortage of ships, fewer goods were imported and by February 1915 various commodities had increased in price. At the end of 1916, Germany was beginning to recognise that she could not win the war on the Western Front and decided to seek victory by waging unrestricted submarine warfare in the Atlantic to starve Britain into submission. By the winter of 1916-17, German U-boats had declared unrestricted warfare on merchant ships and German submarines had sunk 632,000 tons in intensified submarine blockades. When in April 1917 one ship out of four leaving Britain's ports never returned, British shipping losses reached its peak, losing 526,000 tons - the highest loss in any month of the War, Britain's food situation became serious, almost starving Britain into defeat.

Britain imported much of the food needed for her population of around 45,000,000. This position remained secure as long as the Navy could ensure safe transit from suppliers oversees. The local paper,

The Advertiser and Gazette, was amongst the first of the journals to advocate compulsory rationing.

British wheat acreage and production had declined significantly since 1861 and wheat prices fell steadily from the spring of 1915 but when supplies fell seriously short owing to a poor world harvest and following the closure of the Dardanelles, Russian wheat could not be obtained. In 1916, British wheat-fields had been reduced further by a quarter of a million acres and the general production of home-grown food had fallen twelve per cent between 1915 and 1916. Not for 100 years had the price of wheat, barley and oats been so high as in early 1918. The Government had to fix prices. For the first time queues appeared at shops, but this was not on a large scale despite the influx of people to work and to shelter from air-raids.

Although controls on food had begun at an early stage in the War, by 1916 there was no real shortage of food in Britain although prices and wages had begun to rise. By 1916, however, food substitutes were used to a limited extent and by the end of that year, less food was being produced than before the war and although the convoy system cut the sinking of our ships, our food supplies were insufficient to go round at reasonable prices. The poor potato harvest of 1916 reduced the poorer people to hardship and on January 13th 1917, the first food riot occurred. In 1917 despite the crisis in food supply, there was an unwillingness to bring in rationing. By this time the average working-class family needed at least an extra 15 shillings to pay for food and a further 1s 10d per week for rising fuel costs. As part of the Food for Britain Campaign, food parcels were sent out from all over Australia for distribution amongst widows.

Farmers and farmhands had been gradually called up and not much food was being produced. Further, so many people had come not only to work in the area, but refugees, billeted soldiers, wounded men in hospital etc., that there was not enough food to go round. Queues grew more frequent and prices rose. As time went along people became anxious and appeals were made for voluntary rationing. By mid April 1917 the King, Queen and Royal Household had adopted a policy of voluntary rationing and, inspired by this, the people who followed wore a badge of purple ribbon. Lord Devonport, a rich grocer, head of Kearley and Tonge's (provision merchants) and since 1909 Chairman of the Port of London Authority and native of Uxbridge, was appointed the first Food Controller at the Ministry of Food in December 1916 and quickly put into place the restriction of the price of food and launched a voluntary rationing scheme in late May 1917. Mr. J. McCallum was the Food Controller for Harefield.

At the end of May 1917 a food economy campaign was started at Uxbridge and in the months following, demonstrations of appetizing meatless dishes were given. The first national rationing scheme, applying to sugar (two-thirds of which had come from Germany and Austria-Hungary), came into force on 1st March 1917 and again reduced in July 1917, but throughout that year local authorities introduced rationing schemes of their own. There was a shortage of bacon locally by the beginning of October 1917 as well as tea, bread, margarine, lard, condensed milk, rice, butter, paper and some other commodities. Prices rose.

By 1918 the food situation was at its most serious. Local Food Committees were set up. In the spring of that year the country had only two weeks' supply of food left. Even hospitals and schools suffered. The compulsory rationing of certain foods - meat and bacon, butter and margarine (from the end of 1917 local bakers were already using cocoa-butter as an indifferent substitute to margarine), came into operation in the last week of February 1918 and affected London and Middlesex, Hertfordshire, Essex, Kent and Surrey. Early in April the rest of the country was also rationed. Food was distributed almost equally between the rich and the poor more than ever before. Customers were allotted to particular retailers who would be supplied by a specific wholesaler. Each household was issued with two ration cards, one for butcher's meat and bacon and the other for butter or margarine. It was commonly thought that wartime shortages of food would lead to illnesses and possibly also to early deaths in certain civilian communities.

Rationing was not only confined to food. Coal, which by early 1915 had risen in price by 20%, was another necessary commodity of which there was a shortage in Greater London during the winter of 1916-17, and queues of people, in which children predominated, besieged the coal dealers. Coal rationing was introduced in London in the summer of 1917 and was extended to the rest of the country a year later – the Household Fuel and Lighting Order. The Order applied to all consumers of coal, coke or other fuel for heating, cooking or purposes other than industrial. Wasting cinders was a punishable offence! One way of saving coal was put forward – to fill drainpipes with 1 part cement to 9 parts coal dust, ramming this mixture down and adding water. It was supposed to burn for hours. Church services were confined to daylight hours followed by theatres, cinemas, music halls and restaurants. In the summer of 1916 the Daylight Saving, or Summer Time, came into effect which enabled industries to make fuel savings. Restrictions on petrol were imposed early in the war and became more tightened as hostilities progressed.

By 1916 the cost of paper had almost trebled. On February 14th 1916 the Middlesex Education Committee wrote to all the managers of Council and Non-Provided schools the following letter:- '*In view of the great increase in the price of paper and of the great difficulty which will be experienced in obtaining paper, I am directed by my Committee to ask you to be good enough to instruct your Head Teachers to be as economical as possible when ordering exercise books, drawing books, examination paper etc., and as far as possible to commence using slates in stock at once...*' Instructions were also issued that both sides of the paper were also to be used. School magazines either ceased altogether or became much smaller. By mid 1917 Parish magazines were printed on inferior paper and were reduced in length whilst costing more. In January 1918, because of the enormous increase in the price of raw materials, the local paper increased its cost by ½d to 2d. Parish magazines also became more expensive. National newspapers, which were under Government censorship and monitored to ensure they maintained morale, were in 1918 reduced to 4 pages. Sunday papers had stopped being published by this time.

The 'Evening News' in mid August 1914 had carried advice on the vegetables to plant for food supply to those who had gardens or plots of land.

This advice came from Royal Horticultural Society and was also printed in the local paper. The importance of producing food for others was stressed. Before 1916 allotments were virtually unknown but by Christmas 1916 the allotment campaign was well under way, spurred on by the gravity of the food situation. The Government issued a Cultivation of Lands Order facilitating the acquisition of land for smallholdings and market gardens in January 1917. With this Order, Parish Councils and Urban District Councils scheduled land for cultivation after touring the locality. It was thought that some land would be suitable for farmers, for allotments or as grazing land although sometimes it meant that new fencing would be needed which was not available. War Agricultural Committees were set up in each area and a parallel, the Board of Agriculture, set up similar committees in each of the boroughs of the country. They were free to choose their own titles and were formed by and under the authority of the Borough Councils and UDCs. These committees responded willingly to the guidance of the Central Food Production department at the Board of Agriculture who conferred upon them powers for the acquisition of land, within or without their own urban area for food growing, provided that the land could conveniently be cultivated by persons residing within the urban area. Private gardens were also turned over to vegetable growing. Allotment patrols were organised and growers took turns to guard their own and neighbour's plots.

When in late 1914 there was a huge demand for allotments at Harefield, the Council took over 2 acres, part of Poor's Land in Pinner Road from Mr. Benitt, the tenant. The Council, in early 1915, approached Mr. Billyard Leake for 2 more acres of land adjoining the allotments already in use. All allotments were laid out in 10 pole plots. By January 1917 the rule for allowing only 10 pole plots was rescinded and more land to cultivate was wanted. Shortly afterwards four extra acres had been laid out in plots and in 1918 a further 2 acres were laid out but this still did not meet the demand. When applications for 15 more allotments were received in early January 1918, Mr. Billyard Leake granted the use of more land near the allotments already in use. By mid February 1918 the boom in allotments at Harefield was still continuing. Allotments were to be no larger than 10 poles. Land at Hill End was acquired in 1918. The Council School at Harefield was cultivating half an acre of land by January 1917 and by March 1918 had 20 poles of their playground under cultivation as well as having taken over two Council allotments. Here by May 1917, 62 poles of allotments were in cultivation by teachers and scholars of the school. 37 poles were in the school grounds and the rest of the land belonged to Harefield Parish Council and in a field. In late January 1918, about 20 Harefield parishioners took part in a draw at the Old Schools for 3 acres of the new allotment plots of mainly 10 poles with several at 20 poles. One acre of land at the Australian Hospital was also devoted to the growing of foodstuffs.

The Southern Federation of Allotment Holders affiliated to the National Union of Allotment Holders covered the area of London and Southern Counties. It was reported in February 1918 that membership in the last month had increased by almost 5,000 to 15, 000 and by the end of hostilities exceeded 40, 000. The demand for houses was so great that in 1920 some allotment holders from all around the Borough were notified that their plots would be required for building purposes and, therefore, their renting the ground would cease.

As the war went on more and more women were required to fill the gaps caused by men going off to war. In February 1916 there was a call for 400,000 women to carry on agricultural work previously carried out by the men who were now being called up for duty. In the summer of 1916 the Minister of Agriculture foresaw a serious shortage of horticultural labour. When in December 1916 new facilities for training women were set up, Mr. Rose of Dews Farm was approached by the County and by mid-January 1917, the girls' agricultural school at the farm had been set up. Also in that January when a new Minister took office, the Women's Land Army was born, funded by the Government. The Land Army was divided into 3 sections-agricultural, timber cutting and forage (for army horses). Women signed on for either 6 months or a year. If an application was successful the Government offered an initial wage of 20s a week and a free uniform. After passing an efficiency test the wage was raised by 2s a week. Women were expected to go to whichever part of the country the Selection Board thought most fit. Various training schemes were set up in different parts of the country. By the end of the War there were about 250,000 'land girls'. In 1919 the local paper reported that over 5000 women in the Land Army wished to remain in agriculture.

When war ended the bug for allotments had taken hold and in common with the Second World War, rationing continued long after the conclusion of hostilities and was not fully abolished until 3 years after the war ended.

FUND RAISING and COMFORTS

From the moment war was declared, funds for this and that were started, far too many to mention here. Even before the National Relief Fund was developed, a Relief Fund was opened for Middlesex, which was divided into districts with local sub-committees. Uxbridge district became No. 11 Committee and covered Uxbridge, Cowley, Harefield, Hillingdon, Northolt and Ickenham. These committees were given the power to act at once and dealt with the local effects of the war, including to ensure food supplies and to co-ordinate other aspects of the war effort including the care of the wounded at home. Local funds were opened. Ladies' Committees were set up which in the Uxbridge area divided work into 5 smaller committees to collect money and organise other work. There was a visiting committee, a committee for needlework and food depots. Public houses in the district were supplied with collecting boxes for local relief funds. Eventually local Relief Funds amalgamated into the National Relief Fund, which had been inaugurated by the Prince of Wales and aimed to centralise the work. However, by and large, the anticipated levels of distress were not realised and much of the sums raised went to other causes, mainly the Red Cross.

Work quickly got under way to raise money for good causes, knit and sew garments for the poor or for the troops, sew bandages for the wounded, prepare parcels for Prisoners of War etc. Working parties were set up all over the place, flag days sprung up for various causes and funds were started to raise money for some or other purpose. Girls knitted socks, mittens, mufflers and helmets for the troops.

War Savings Associations were set up under the National War Savings Committee. Children purchasing War Savings Stamps or subscribing through a War Savings Association, or adults purchasing on behalf of a child, were issued with pictured stamps on demand – one for each 6d spent. The Government spent money on all kinds of things from paying for the war and the reconstruction of housing schemes, health reforms and education after the war as well as for arranging for finding work for demobilised men. The Government continuously borrowed money at short notice by means of Treasury Bills and in order to repay them money was required which could only be obtained by all the citizens of the State continuing to purchase War Savings Certificates and War Bonds.

WOMEN'S WAR WORK SERIES.
No. 16. IN THE ORCHARD.

In order to reduce borrowing and raise funds for the war effort, the Government produced certificates, stamps and posters, sold to the public through a variety of outlets. This is one stamp from the series 'Women's Work in the War'

The absence from home of men on Military Service in many instances left their wives or mothers in a state of economic instability until their separation allowance from the Military Authorities arrived. The children could not be fed. On 7th August 1914, the Education (Provision of Meals) Act became law. It gave a local Education Authority, without any application to the Board of Education, to spend out of the rates such sums as may be necessary to meet the cost of food for children attending public elementary schools within their area on both days when the school meets and on other days. There was a larger amount of distress than at any time in any previous year since free meals were given by the Education Authorities. Very few children whose fathers had enlisted were being fed, although it wasn't usually long before the mother received the separation allowance.

Local offices of The Soldiers' and Sailors' Families Association (SSFA), which for many years had alleviated the difficulties arising where the breadwinner had gone off to war, were started with voluntary staff. Their biggest work was visits and the advancing of money to distressed families until the separation allowance came in. They only dealt with NCOs and men. By the end of 1914 Lady Hillingdon was president for Middlesex, as she had been during the Boer War, with Dr. Christopher Addison of Northwood as vice-president and the Rev. Prebend C.M. Harvey, vicar of Hillingdon, treasurer. The Uxbridge Division of Middlesex covered the whole of the modern London Borough of Hillingdon and also included Cranford and Northolt. No cases from Harefield were dealt with in the first two years of the war. War Pensions Committees were also set up.

The 'Gazette' started a fund for supplying Middlesex 'Tommies' at the front with cigarettes, almost a soon as the broke out. Various other funds were also set up including those for soldiers and sailors, Prisoners of War and Belgian refugees.

Mrs. Clark, tobacconist of Harefield suggested collecting cigarettes and tobacco in boxes for the soldiers. Civilians, firms and schoolchildren all helped to contribute towards these funds, amongst them were the workers at the United Asbestos Co. at Harefield who contributed weekly to support refugees and the scholars of the Council schools had by mid October 1915 spent upwards of £30.00 in material making comforts for the soldiers.

DEFENCE

Much of the bombing of Britain was indiscriminate, although military targets were in most cases sought. Usually the bombing was sporadic with only the occasional sustained bombing. Nevertheless there were a considerable number of casualties and heavy material damage. Although fewer bombs were dropped by aeroplanes than by airships, more casualties and damage were caused by them. This was probably because attacks by aeroplanes were directed towards cities and towns, whereas airships dropped many bombs indiscriminately from great heights – and often in open country in order to lighten airships.

By August 1914 only 30 Anti-Aircraft (AA) guns were deployed in the United Kingdom, and 25 of these were 1-pounder 'pom-poms' – remnants from the Boer War. In London there was an old 'pom pom' and a naval 6-pounder, very clumsily mounted. At the end of October 1914 the Royal Artillery were placed in charge of defending everywhere but the capital and the Admiralty was confirmed in the responsibility for the defence of London – aeroplanes, guns and searchlights, temporarily assisted by four Royal Flying Corps aircraft from Joyce Green at Dartford and Hounslow, two at each, of other large undefended towns and for dealing with enemy aircraft crossing the coast. Military airships also guarded London

After an airship raid on London, the city's first, on the night of 31st May/1st June 1915 killing seven people, other 3-inch guns increased London defences to eight. Until 1917 there were only 16 guns, comprised of AA Defence Force fixed gun and searchlight positions, the Royal Naval Anti-Aircraft Mobile Brigade with, eventually, 14 guns mounted on lorries and another mobile force equipped only with light AA guns, defending London, mostly manned by Royal National Volunteer Reservists (RNVR) part-timers.

The deficiency in these defences was emphasised by the raids of September 1915. On 1st October 1915 orders were issued by the Admiralty for guns, searchlights and aeroplanes to be brought to London as a precautionary measure against aerial attacks. Northolt Aerodrome along with Hainault and Sutton's Farm all received two of the very best machines then available - BE (Bleriot Experimental) 2Cs. Searchlights were installed near all aerodromes and mobile guns were also made available. 120 Special Constables were at first deployed to man the searchlights when difficulty was experienced in finding crews.

In September 1916, the country was divided into two AA Defence Zones. The 'Ever Ready Zone', where all defences were in permanently readiness for action covered this area. In April 1917 this Zone was divided and renamed as Zones 'X' and 'Y', and in May 1917, the Army took control of all defences and a 'London Air Defence Area' was created. Rings of defences surrounded the Capital with guns in the central area with an inner ring of AA guns at about a 5 mile radius. A cordon of thirteen-pounder mobile Anti-Aircraft guns and searchlights around the north-western fringes of London surrounded this area where fighter aircraft could patrol. Beyond this arc was a circle of gun defences surrounding the Home Counties, with outlying gun areas in Kent and Essex. Outside this circle was another searchlight ring. London had balloon aprons each consisting of three Caquot captive balloons 500 yards apart and connected by horizontal wire from which was suspended at 25 feet intervals, steel wires 1,000 feet in length. Eventually the height was raised to around 10,000 feet. This forced the raiders to keep above that height and so enable the defending machines the more easily to hunt them. Gun defence Sub-Commands were formed and from 1917 to 1918, London's Western Sub-Command, which covered this area, consisted of 19 gun stations with twelve fixed 75mm French guns on mounts, four 'mobile' 75mm French auto-canons and three 3-inch calibre British anti-aircraft guns and 36 searchlight stations, which extended from about 2 miles beyond Watford to 3 miles south of Bromley and from Windsor to Grove Park. The Sub-Command HQ was established in the Metropolitan Waterworks at Putney Heath. Each gun-station was under the charge of an officer and manned by a sergeant, a corporal and between 16 and 18 men. There were double crews at each station in order that the crews could work on alternate nights. Central stations (such as Hyde Park, Paddington

Recreation Ground, Parliament Hill and Deptford) remained in the charge of the RNVR. Beyond them was a ring of inner guns, such as Richmond, Hounslow, Hanwell, Acton, Horsenden Hill and Kenton, with an outer ring extending through Eastcote, Windsor, Staines, Hampton, Morden, Croydon and Bromley to Grove Park.

In the summer of 1917, 90 Fire Brigades in an area of 750 square miles were organised to give aid in London in any emergency. All Reservists were called up from the front and engineer detachments attached to the firemen were doubled. When the first air-raid warning reached the Fire Brigade its supports closed in from the outlying area towards the most dangerous points.

The defence of London never did reach its intended potential, unlike Paris which, after a raid on January 29th 1916 which killed 26 people, thereafter developed its defences so well that the French capital was left unassailed by Zeppelins.

POLICE

The existing police forces of the country, which had largely recruited men discharged from the fighting services, had suddenly been deprived of the services of all their Reservists, both Army and Navy. Not only was the strength of the regular constabulary reduced and efforts were made to spread their work amongst those of their colleagues left behind, but the duties devolved to the Police during wartime became more numerous and varied as we have seen. In the Metropolitan area, all police leave was cancelled for the first year.

As it was at the time of the Boer War, it was these types of men, those above military age, those in some essential occupation and men physically unfit for war services who were encouraged to volunteer as Special Constables, an amateur service created by the War.

This new service sprang into action at the outbreak of war and all strata of society turned up in their numbers to enlist. By 24th August 1914, 20,000 men and by the end of 1914, 31,000 men had enrolled and were given the same powers, duties and privileges as a regular policeman. They had to take the King's Oath and were issued with a constable's warrant and a whistle. At first they wore a blue and white armlet and some months later were issued with a blue uniform cap. A uniform came later still but only after a certain number of drills and duty 'turns' had been completed.

Colonel Sir Edward Ward, Bart, Permanent Under-Secretary of State, War Office, 1901-1914, inspecting the 'X' Division of the Special Police at Blackheath (H.W. Wilson, The Great War)

A Special Constabulary Force for the whole of the London Metropolitan Police district, an area which embraced all the environs of London and all

London itself apart from the City was amongst the very first to be established. There were 21 divisions in the Metropolitan Police district of which most of the local area formed part of the Northern District in 'X' Division. However, it is possible Harefield was outside the Metropolitan area. They began their monotonous duties late in August 1914 and undertook night duties at vulnerable positions. Scotland Yard suggested that all Council workers be enrolled as Special Constables for the purpose of protecting Council property.

The Special Constabulary were also occasionally called on to attend in London in order to relieve the London 'Specials' during and after air-raids and in October 1917 were provided with steel helmets to protect them from the hail of steel fragments scattered by anti-aircraft guns. (H.W. Wilson, The Great War)

Each Metropolitan Police Division had its own motor-transport section and a fleet of London buses was given to the Metropolitan Police force to facilitate the transport of police between divisions when the need arose. A third of the number was always on duty and available for service. Thus, at a moment's notice, at a call for police into any of the London divisions, a hundred or more buses, if need be, could set off without delay to bring in police from other divisions. On Saturday 7th July 1917 when a fleet of nearly 30 German aeroplanes flying in duck formation raided London, Special Police in their hundreds were collected from the division and despatched to East London, where the damage was the greatest.

As time went on, the duties of the 'Specials' changed considerably. They became efficient and available in first-aid work. During the air-raids the police would have hardly coped but for the Specials who were always on duty helping patrol the streets for any signs of light, arranging the 'take cover' notices etc. In 1916 it was the Special Constabulary in one of their vehicles who transported the traitor, Roger Casement, across London to Brixton Prison. By August 1917, London's Special Constables had taken over from the military people the manning of observation posts.

Growing industrial unrest in July 1918 caused widespread strikes. In August 1918 there was a strike of 11,000 London tram and bus workers for more pay for women workers. So suddenly and unexpected, on the night of August 30th about 14,000 Metropolitan Police stopped work for an increase in pay, including their war bonus, and for their union to be officially recognised. Not a single policeman was on beat duty and only a handful was out controlling traffic. The 'Specials' had been called out, but according to common report the response was rather half-hearted. Although this strike went on for nearly 3 days there was no increase in the crime levels. Their demands for more pay were met.

Although Special Constable duty ceased on 23rd November 1918, in March 1919 the local Special Constabulary were on special duty in London at the funeral of Nurse Edith Cavell. She had been shot as a spy by the Germans at the beginning of August 1915 and buried where she fell. On March 17th 1919, her body was exhumed and brought back to England for reburial at Norwich Cathedral.

In early October 1921, Special Constables were honoured in Hyde Park when the Duke of York presented long-service medals to members of the Metropolitan Special Constabulary. Every man who had served in the Force during the war and had put in at least 150 duties, was entitled to the medal. Service in the then present reserve also counted but it had to be three times the length of that required in the war force. The officers and men present, 5,000 strong, represented 24 police divisions. All the chief officers of the 'X' Division were present. After an inspection of the whole reserve, the Duke of York handed out medals to staff, divisional and senior station officers. At the same time commandants handed medals at tables near by to the inspectors and sub inspectors who in turn distributed them to the men on parade. Chief Inspector W.O. Lovibond received his medal from the Duke of York and the medals to sub inspectors Woodbridge, Winstone and Stagg were pinned on by Commander Inston. The medals to the men were presented by the chief inspectors of each section.

SCOUTS
Most of the local Scoutmasters were called to active service with the Territorials on 19th August 1914. They were under the personal direction of the

74

District Commissioner. Each scoutmaster was instructed to prepare lists of scouts willing to mobilize for action. The local police received a copy of these lists. A general circular from the Chief Scout described the possible duties of the Scouts volunteering for service. Their duties were not of a military nature but of a material service to the country – communications, guarding bridges and other vulnerable places, collecting information on transport, acting as guides and orderlies, forwarding dispatches dropped by aircraft, etc. Sea Scouts were to watch estuaries and ports, guide vessels in unbuoyed channels, showing lights to friendly vessels etc. The local Scouts were placed at the disposal of the police and the Council Relief Committee and those on Government or special duty would be on a ration allowance. A shilling a day was allowed to each officer and Scout employed, but District Commissioners were requested to keep the expenses down where possible as the headquarters fund was limited. Each Scout in uniform also had to wear the fleur de lys buttonhole badge. This was mandatory in order to be recognized as members of the association.

The Scout and Guide movements had great appeal during World War One. Scouts were active throughout the war. Within the first few hours after war was declared the Scouts had taken up the duty of guarding important railway bridges, water-works and telegraph and cable lines throughout the country – day and night. The Army and the Territorial troops later relieved them. They patrolled cliffs with coastguards and provided a messenger service for the police, stood guard over strategic bridges and telephone lines and had bugles to alert the public sheltering from Zeppelins and aircraft that all was now clear. Guides carried out tasks such as helping out in canteens, helping in hospitals, including acting as stretcher-bearers and first-aiders. They also entertained. Scouts who carried out war service of one kind or another were awarded a little strip of red material with a yellow date on it, which was worn on the right breast.

REFUGEES and EVACUEES

During September 1914, a constant stream of Belgian refugee poured into England. By direction of the authorities, the refugees were quarantined and vaccinated. At first they arrived at Folkestone but in October, when it was seen that the German army would soon reach the coast, many thousands arrived at Dover. On their arrival in London they were taken to a temporary haven in Aldwych. In the seven days beginning with 10th October, some 13,000 arrived, including 5,000 wounded Belgian soldiers. Within days of the outbreak of war preparations were being made to receive Belgian refugees, who in most cases were panic-stricken and had lost everything. Everywhere, doors were flung wide open to receive the destitute refugees. Thousands of offers poured in from people willing to house and feed them. Local houses were rented for the refugee families from the early days of the war and furnished by contributions and residents loaned a great deal of furniture. Councils excused properties occupied by the refugees, who worked for their livelihood and supported themselves, from paying rates.

The difficulties of classifying and registering the thousands of offers, the fitting of the guests to the hosts in batches of twos and threes, the temporary housing, the final dispatch of the refugees to country districts, all involved an immense labour. Local committees were formed, and there were soon 2,000 of them. Refugees were picked up from Aldwych where the Belgium Consulate had, early in the war, opened an office in General Buildings. Volunteer motorists conveyed many to their new homes. These volunteers became the Optimistic National Corps, Transport Section, then the Motor Squadron of the London Volunteer Rifles and eventually the National Motor Volunteers.

At Harefield, one of the places used to house Belgians was the Memorial Hall. A family of five refugees were also guests of Mrs. Tarleton and the employees of the Breakspeare estate at Wickham Lodge on the Pinner Road. It was furnished by the residents of the Breakspear estate and received the refugees in late November 1914. Several of the refugees were employed at the asbestos works in Harefield, as were some of the refugees who were also housed at the Memorial Hall. A family of five refugees arrived in early 1915 as guests of the employees of Messrs. Coles, Shadbolt & Co., and quartered in a house opposite the 'Halfway House'.

About 100,000 Belgians fled to England after Germany invaded their country. These refugees did not establish new homes for themselves after the War but went back to Belgium.

PRISONERS OF WAR

Prisoners of War were numbered in the millions and there were many charges on both sides that the rules, drawn up at an international conference at The Hague in 1899 and 1907, were not being observed. The exact number of local men taken prisoner is difficult to establish. Some of them died from disease, starvation or dysentery. Civilians working abroad were also liable to be captured. In the spring of 1918 during the German spring offensive many local lads were captured. Among them was Cuthbert. L. Ogg (Black Watch) of Harefield, who had been educated at Harefield School and who worked for the Asbestos Company for 13 years before relinquishing his position in May 1916 to take up Military duty. He also played football for the Breakspear Institute at some time. George Hampstead who lived with his family in one of the cottages adjoining the 'Spotted Dog' at Harefield had served during the war for almost 2½ years with the Buffs, but for a considerable time was a POW. He had received a blow on his head whilst a POW for refusing to work in a munition factory. Since then he had suffered from nose-bleeds. He death in early 1922 was attributed to his neglect during the war, dysentery etc.

After the armistice, those captured gradually returned home and celebrations were held everywhere to welcome home returning servicemen.

Local Prisoners of War Funds were set up early in the War, affiliated to the British Red Cross Fund through its Central Prisoner of War Committee. It was agreed that properly selected food should be sent to each prisoner once a fortnight and parcel should weigh 10lb with 13 lb. of bread. Although food parcels were sent to the men, it is doubted whether all were received. Unless a special label was affixed to the parcel, no Post Office would accept it and no individual could hand over a parcel there. In 1917 it was agreed that private parcels of food and clothing weighing up to 11lb from family and friends was allowed. Northwood Fund, which was registered under the War Charities Act 1916, began in June 1915, secured the responsibility of supplying parcels to prisoners in the Middlesex Regiment. It was the only centre for distribution in the whole of Middlesex. In the period beginning June 1915 and ending in December 1916 they had despatched 12 large cases and 750 parcels of food to 37 different prisoners, averaging one parcel per fortnight per prisoner. During 1917, 864 parcels were sent. By June 1918 £1170 had been collected together with gifts in kind and 72 parcels had been dispatched to 12 POWs that year. In May 1918 there was an appeal signed by the Duke of Bedford urging the claims of the Lord Lieutenant's County Fund for Middlesex Regiment's Prisoners of War of which there were 1,400 by the beginning of 1918. £17,000 was needed to support them.

PEOPLE

Private Cecil John Kinross VC., 49th Battalion, Canadian Infantry, won his VC in a gallant charge of a machine gun which was causing great loss at Passchendaele on 30th October 1917. Early in the advance of his company they came under intense artillery fire and were then held up by machine-guns. Kinross rose up among the remains of his comrades in full view of the enemy. Headless of the shrapnel, high explosive and machine-gun bullets, he searched the distance for the machine-gun causing the greatest loss. On finding it he removed his equipment until he only carried a cotton bandolier and his rifle with bayonet fixed. Alone he walked across the open ground separating him from the machine-gun, which poured out a wild stream of fire around him. As he got close to the gun he rushed. There followed a brief fight and he killed the crew of six and destroyed the gun. His example and courage enabled a further advance of 300 yards to be made and a highly important position to be established. He was wounded later in the day. Details differ, but it seems that he was probably born at Uxbridge on 17th February 1895 and had lived for a time at Highway Farm, Harefield. He died in Alberta, Canada, on 21st June 1957.

Mr. (Commander) A.H. Tarleton, RN of Harefield, Chief Commissioner of the County Boy Scouts, who was on the Royal Navy emergency list.

Robert Ryder was born in Harefield on 17th December 1895, son of Robert Edward Ryder of Breakspear Road. He had attended Harefield School and prior to joining up had worked at the Asbestos Mill. He enlisted in the 12th Middlesex Regiment at the outbreak of war at Mill Hill. He had already been recommended for bravery in the Battle of the Somme in July 1916 when he was awarded to Victoria Cross for bravery at Thiepval on September 26th 1916. Zero hour was fixed for 12.35pm, rather than the usual attack at dawn. The battalion had moved out at Zero hour to capture Thiepval village. His company was held up by heavy rifle fire and all of his officers had become casualties. There was confusion as without any officer the attack was flagging. Private Ryder dashed alone at the enemy trench and by skilful manipulations of his Lewis gun, succeeded in clearing the trench. When news of his award reached Harefield, the pupils at Harefield School were given a day's holiday. On his return to the front he was greeted all the way from Denham Station and was saluted by the wounded Australians from the ANZAC Hospital.

ARMISTICE! - Monday 11th NOVEMBER 1918

On Monday 11th November 1918, the day of the Armistice, it was dreary and wet. Hostilities in the west had ceased at 11am French time, but the last four years, fourteen weeks and two days had taught everyone to be patient. Many false hopes and rumours had circulated before. Eleven o'clock came and went. A surprising silence had descended when suddenly guns, hooters, horns etc blared. Just before midday, as news of the armistice spread workmen downed tools and most school children were given a half-day holiday. Joyful crowds full of hysterical jubilation were cheering, whistling and singing and commandeered vehicles of every description. Drapers were besieged with people buying Union Jacks, which they hung from bedroom windows. All kinds of musical instruments appeared as if by magic. Patriotic songs were the order of the day. This good-natured rowdyism lasted until the Saturday night. Perhaps the most striking thing was the lighted streets and no worry about Special Constables coming to knock at the door. Huge bonfires were lit after dark, but it started raining heavily and the fires were put out.

Flags promptly appeared. The Asbestos Works almost closed down on hearing the news. An attempt was made to start work on the following day but as there were too many absentees it did not re-open for business until 14th November. At the Australian Hospital drinking was the order of the day and the schoolchildren marched through the streets.

The guns had fallen silent. The 'war to end all wars' was over and peace was here at long last but the cost had been high. Death on such a scale had never been witnessed before. Almost 1,000,000 Britons has lost their lived. Civilian losses, apart from those who perished in air-raids, amounted to 15,000 deaths among the crews and passengers of merchant and shipping vessels. Miss J. Coster, a native of Chorley Wood who lived at Harefield with her married sister when she was in England, was a stewardess with the P. and O. 'Persia', a Royal Mail steamer. She had been with the P. and O. company for 12 years and was killed when the steamer was torpedoed and rapidly sunk (within 5 minutes) by German submarine U-38 off Crete on 30th December 1915. No warning had been given.

Everywhere things gradually began to turn back to normal, although some things that had been abandoned never returned and others took some time to return. For instance, the choirs of St. Margaret's, Uxbridge, and St. Andrew's, Uxbridge, St. John's Uxbridge Moor, Cowley, Yiewsley, West Drayton, Harmondsworth, Harlington Hayes, Ruislip and Harefield had met annually for a festival service at Hillingdon on St. John the Baptist day – June 24th. They had last met in 1913 and did not reconvene until 1923.

Of the seven million men who went to fight, a tenth of them never returned – almost a whole generation had been wiped out. The War Memorials shows that Harefield lost 68 (or 78) men in this War, 10 had worked on the Breakspear estate.

Their names will live forevermore.

THE WAR MEMORIALS

Harefield War Memorial

In late 1920 Harefield Council approached the Middlesex County Council with a view of obtaining a site for the memorial in the grounds of Harefield Park, facing the common, rather than place it at the corner of the common. The memorial, designed by Mr. F. Herbert Mansford of Ruislip, stands on Harefield Green commemorating the First World War dead from that village, and is in the form of an obelisk of Portland Stone, about 22 feet tall. A raised laurel lead adorns each side. The memorial was erected facing the pond and commemorates the 78 men from the parish who were never to return from World War One. Prebendary G.H. Vincent dedicated the obelisk on a Sunday in July 1921, which stands on a pedestal bearing the names of the fallen. Around it is a pavement of flagstones and pebbles.

The east and south faces of the memorial are dedicated to World War One casualties and the north face, to those 35 men from the parish who died during the Second World War, unveiled on Remembrance Sunday 1948.

Harefield Memorial Plaque, St. Mary's Church

At the top of the marble plaque, at the western end of the nave, is an inscription with the names of the fallen of World War One underneath. To the right of the marble plaque is a wooden plaque, carved and decorated, also commemorating World War One and also World War Two.

A hand drawn calf-bound book, with pen and ink illustrations also commemorates World War One.

Another plaque, in highly polished marble in the Churchyard commemorating Gerald Littlehayes Goodlake, the first VC, which was awarded by Queen Victoria in Hyde Park, for services in the Crimea. He held Windmill Ravine against a much larger force. He also received another medal with 4 clasps, Sebastopol, Alma, Inkerman and Balaclava. He lived at Denham Fishery and was buried at Harefield.

Australian War Memorial, Harefield

The unveiling and dedication of the war memorial placed in the Churchyard of St. Mary's Church to the memory of the Australian soldiers who died in hospital at Harefield took place on Sunday 13th November 1921 at 3.15pm. The Archbishop of Melbourne dedicated the granite obelisk and the unveiling ceremony was performed by the Agent-Generals of Western Australia and Tasmania, and Sir Ross Smith, an airman who flew with his brother from England to Australia. The cemetery is entered through an archway of Portland stone. A map of the cemetery is in St. Mary's Church and shows the location of the graves.

A 'wheel', signed by all of those Australians who remained in the hospital after war ended, can be found in Uxbridge Local Studies Library.

On 28th April 1929, a marble tablet placed at the western end of the nave, in memory of the 112 Australian soldiers buried in Harefield Churchyard, presented to the Church by Sir Francis Newdigate, GCMG, patron of the living, was unveiled by Major-General the Hon. Sir Granville de Laune Kyrie, KCMG,CB, High Commissioner of Australia.

In April 1950, the Australian Chapel of Remembrance was dedicated by the Lord Bishop of London, the service of which was broadcast by the BBC to Australia and New Zealand at the Annual Commemoration of Anzac Day at Harefield Church. Following the dedication, the Lord Lieutenant of the County, Lord Latham, unveiled a plaque inscribed: This chapel is dedicated to the Glory of God and to the memory of the men and women of Australia fighting forces who gave their lives in the cause of freedom, 1914-18, 1939-1945'. Also in that year, the flag which flew over the Australian Hospital during the 1914-1918 war was presented to St. Mary's Church and hangs in the memorial chapel.

HAREFIELD WAR MEMORIAL (ORGAN)

An organ and screen built in St. Mary's Church in 1952 is in memory of those who died in the 1939-1945 war. The old organ had been in use for over 100 years and was replaced by an electrically pumped organ which was installed by Messrs. Davies and Son. The organ case is in oak with a bronze plaque attached with the names of the 38 dead inscribed. It was dedicated on Monday 23rd June 1952, by the former vicar, the Rev. K. Toole Mackson, followed by a recital by Mr. Brian Trant, sometime organist at St. Andrew's Church, Uxbridge.

HAREFIELD WESLEYAN CHURCH

The Church was there at Harefield by 1871, but demolished in 1985 or 1986. A Roll of Honour 1939-1945, stored in Christ Church, Uxbridge, commemorates 'the sons and daughters of members' who went off to fight, but who returned. Fifteen names are recorded together with their regimental numbers and rank.

An identical Roll of Honour, without any names, commemorates World War One:-

HAREFIELD METHODIST CHURCH
In Memory
To the men
Of gave
Their lives
And served
In the
1914-1918
War

In about 1922, a small two-manual, hand-blown tracker organ was installed in the Chapel of the Methodist Church as a memorial to those who had worshipped at there and who were killed or died of wounds in the First World War. After it arrived from its former home, gaily painted, it was painted deep brown and grained, more in keeping for its purpose.

The Rolls of Honour commemorating both World Wars are now kept at Christ Church, Redford Way, Uxbridge.

BELLS UNITED ASBESTOS COMPANY

Bell's War Memorial, originally erected in the company's premises at Harefield, was moved after the business was sold, to the Parish Church of St.

Mary, and unveiled and dedicated on the evening of 12th April 1930, amongst an exceptionally large congregation. Many of the workers commemorated lived around West Hyde in Hertfordshire.

BREAKSPEAR ESTATE MEMORIAL

At the beginning of June 1919, a memorial service was carried out in Harefield Church to commemorate the ten men killed out of those who went to war from Breakspears estate. In the Breakspears Chapel a brass tablet was unveiled and dedicated by the Bishop of Kensington. The inscription read: 'To the glory of Almighty God and in eternal memory of the following from the Breakspears Estate, who laid down their lives for their King and Country in the Great War 1914-1918: Thomas Cooper, Thomas Cullen, Joseph Henry Heard, Edwin Lawrence Humphreys, Percy Lamb, George William Lamb, Walter Forsyth Marshall, George Marshall, Sidney Purser, Charles Edwin Watkins. On whose souls, Jesus, have mercy on them, Amen'. The service was conducted by the Right Reverend the Bishop of Kensington, assisted by the Rev. Albert Augustus Harland, Vicar of Harefield, and the Rev. W. Russell acting as Chaplain to the Bishop.

INDEX OF NAMES

BIBLIOGRAPHY

ADAM-SMITH, P. The Anzacs. Hamish Hamilton, 1978

BENNETT, L.G. The horticultural industry of Middlesex. University of Reading, 1952

BINGHAM, S. Ministering angels. Osprey, 1979

BOURNE, J. Britain and the Great War 1914-1918. Edward Arnold, 1994

Capital Cities at War: Paris, London, Berlin, 1914-1919, edited by Jay Winter and Jean-Louis Robert. Cambridge, 1999

COLE, C. The air defence of Britain 1914-1918. Putman, 1984

COLE, G.D.H. Workshop Organisation. Oxford (Clarendon Press), 1923

GILLMAN, P. Collar the lot! How Britain interned and expelled its wartime refugees. Quartet Books, 1980

GEORGE, D.L. War memories of David Lloyd George. Volume II. Ivor Nicholson and Watson. 1933

Harefield − 'at that time of day': life in a Middlesex village 1800 to the 1930s. Harefield Local History Society, 1978
1
Harefield History Society Newsletter No. 32. Autumn 1996

KAYE, P. Under an English heaven. P. Kaye, 1993

KING, P. Women rule the plot: the story of the 100 year fight to establish women's place in farm and garden. Duckworth, 1999

McMILLAN, J. The way it was 1914-1934. William Kimber and Co. Ltd., 1979

MORRIS, J. The German air raids on Great Britain 1914-1918. H. Pordes, 1969

PLUMRIDGE, J.H. Hospital ships and ambulance trains. Seeley, Service & Co., 1975

PRATT, E.A. British railways and the Great War. Selwyn and Blount, 1921

Prisoners of War Bureau. List of places of internment. No date

RAWLINSON, A. The defence of London, 1915-1918. Andrew Melrose, 1924

ROBINSON, D.H. The Zeppelin in combat: a history of the German Naval Airship Division, 1912-1918. G.T. Foulis, 1971

ROSCOE, T. The history of Harefield compiled for wounded Australians at Harefield Park Hospital.

SHEPHERD, M.P. Heart of Harefield: the story of a hospital. Quiller Press, 1990

SOUTHERTON, P. The story of a prison. Osprey, 1975

TAYLOR, A.J.P. English history 1914-1945. Oxford at the Clarendon Press, 1976

The Times History of the War. The Times 1914-1919

TWINCH, C. Women on the land: their story during two world wars. Lutterworth Press, 1990

TYACK, G. Life and work in a Middlesex village: Harefield 1880-1914. Hillingdon Borough Libraries, 1984

WILLIAMS, J. The home fronts: Britain, France and Germany 1914-1918. Constable, 1972

WILSON, T. The Myriad faces of war: Britain and the Great War 1914-1918. Polity Press, 1988

WINTER, J.M. The Great War and the British People. Palgrave Macmillan, 2003.

Soldiers' and Sailors' Families Associations pamphlets 1914-c1916

The Middlesex County Times 1913-1950